BITCOIN BASICS

101 Questions and Answers

Eric Sammons

Copyright © 2015 Eric Sammons

Published by Saragossa Press, Venice, Florida.
www.saragossapress.com

All rights reserved.

ISBN: 0692572333
ISBN-13: 978-0692572337

Cover design by Grove Street Design Studio.

DEDICATION

For my dad,
who was the first to teach me
the value of money.

CONTENTS

Introduction 1

Bitcoin Basics 5

Bitcoin as a Payment Network 11

Bitcoin as Currency 21

Ownership of Bitcoin Network 25

Technological Advantages of Bitcoin 29

Economic Advantages of Bitcoin 35

Using Bitcoin 47

Cost of Using Bitcoin 61

Bitcoin Mining 65

Anonymity of Using Bitcoin 71

Security of Bitcoin 75

Value of Bitcoin 79

Objections to Bitcoin 83

The Future of Bitcoin 87

Conclusion 91

Resources 93

INTRODUCTION

I remember the first time I ever sent an email. The year was 1992, and I was sitting in front of a terminal hooked to a mainframe in my college computer lab. The entire experience was text-based – no graphics, no mouse, no "send" button to click. Everything had to be typed in – the recipient email address, the text, and even the command to send. I sent the email to one of the few people I knew who had an email address – a fellow Systems Analysis major. The whole affair was underwhelming. And when I tried to explain the concept of email to some of my non-technical friends, I was met mostly with blank stares. "Why do you need to send someone a message like that – can't you just call them?" "That seems really complicated – why bother?" If I had told them that within a decade sending an email would be as familiar as turning on the TV, most of them would have been highly skeptical.

Bitcoin today is like email in the early 90's – and it has the potential to be as much a part of our life in the future as email is today. Since its origin in 2008, its popularity has exploded. Now economists, venture capitalists, financial executives, and even some politicians are embracing what a few years ago was a fringe interest of a handful of technical hobbyists. Nevertheless most "regular" people have no idea what Bitcoin is, even if they've heard of it. They might have some vague impressions – "Isn't that like Internet money?" or "Don't people buy drugs with that?" – but they don't really understand Bitcoin, or why anyone would be interested in using it, or how to use it themselves.

That is the purpose of this book. If you are one of those "regular" people who is interested in Bitcoin but doesn't know where to start, then this book will help you navigate this quickly developing technology.

Perhaps you're already familiar with Bitcoin. If you bring up Bitcoin to a friend, and he gives you a quizzical look, hand him this book. If you mention Bitcoin at your family Thanksgiving dinner, and your cousin says, "I don't really understand that," send her a copy of this book.

Although this book explains the technical and economic ideas behind Bitcoin, it is intended for the non-technician, the non-economist. Anyone who knows how to use email and how to pay for something online with a credit card can read this book profitably. Some parts of the book cover the more practical aspects of Bitcoin – how to spend and receive it, how to store it, etc. – and other parts explain the reasons behind the creation of Bitcoin and the problems it is intended to solve. You only need to know the former to use Bitcoin, but knowing the latter can give you a leg up in becoming knowledgeable about this new and exciting phenomenon.

No one knows the future of Bitcoin, but it has the potential to do for money what the Internet has done for communications. And if this happens, everyone will need to understand at least the basics of Bitcoin. This little book will help you do that.

How to Use This Book

You can get a lot out of this book by simply reading it from cover to cover – the questions are ordered in such a way that they build upon previous questions as much as possible.

Like any discussion of a complicated topic, however, the progress of our investigation of Bitcoin is not always linear. Often a topic is brought up in answering one question that will not be fully explained until later in the book. In addition some readers will want to skip to the questions of most interest to them rather than reading cover to cover. For these reasons we have provided graphics in the form of an arrow that will help you to navigate the material in the book as you read.

Some readers may be looking for a quick start – "Tell me how to use it first and I'll get to the rest later." In this case, read the following chapters first: *Bitcoin Basics*, *Using Bitcoin*, *Cost of Using Bitcoin*, and *Security of Bitcoin*. Once you're up and running refer back to the remaining chapters to gain a fuller understanding of Bitcoin.

BITCOIN BASICS

1. What is Bitcoin?

Bitcoin is a decentralized global monetary system comprised of both an electronic payment network and the digital currency used on that network. In today's world, payment networks and currencies are usually

> Don't worry about being confused at this point – these terms will all be explained in the following chapters!

separate; for example, dollars, euros, and yen are currencies, and credit cards make up payment networks that allow you to spend those currencies more easily. However, with Bitcoin the network and currency combine into one integrated system. The system resides entirely on the Internet and takes full advantage of its power and global reach.

2. Who created Bitcoin?

Satoshi Nakamoto is the creator of Bitcoin. "Satoshi Nakamoto" is likely a pseudonym for the person, or persons, who invented it. Nakamoto's true identity is a mystery, and he (or she or the group) has not been involved in Bitcoin since 2010. Some people are uneasy about the mysterious origins of Bitcoin, but as we will see, Bitcoin was created precisely so that it would not have to be owned or managed by any one person or entity.

3. When was Bitcoin created?

Satoshi released a white paper online in November 2008 that first introduced the concept of Bitcoin. In January 2009, Satoshi released the first code for using Bitcoin and started the network by "mining" the first bitcoins.

> Mining will be described in the chapter *Bitcoin Mining*.

4. When did the first "real-world" Bitcoin transaction occur?

Bitcoin was first used in a "real-world" transaction (the purchase of something of known value) on May 22, 2010. On that day, a programmer named Laszlo Hanyecz paid 10,000 bitcoins to a fellow Bitcoin user for two Papa John's pizzas. Many Bitcoin enthusiasts now celebrate May 22 as "Bitcoin Pizza Day." Hanyecz's pizza order inaugurated the use of Bitcoin in everyday transactions.

5. Why was Bitcoin created?

As both an electronic payment system and a currency, Bitcoin was created to resolve problems of both a technological and an economic nature. Technologically, Bitcoin addresses the inefficiencies of traditional payment systems, such as expensive transaction fees, widespread fraud, and slow money transfers. Economically, Bitcoin addresses the requirement of a trusted third party

> See *Technological Advantages of Bitcoin* and *Economic Advantages of Bitcoin* for more details.

for financial transactions as well as government control of the money supply.

6. Why is Bitcoin called a "cryptocurrency?"

Cryptocurrency is a generic term that describes a currency based on cryptography (the science of encryption). Most currencies today are backed by governments, whereas Bitcoin is backed by mathematical protocols.

> Bitcoin protocols will be explained in the chapter *Ownership of the Bitcoin Network*.

7. What is an "alt-coin?"

Since the creation of Bitcoin, many other people and groups have created electronic currencies and payment networks similar to Bitcoin. These alternative systems are generically called "alt-coins" and are also cryptocurrencies. Most alt-coins are simply variations of Bitcoin itself, with minor changes in how they work. These alt-coins will not be covered in this book, but many of the concepts behind them are the same as those behind Bitcoin.

8. Bitcoin seems confusing – is it just for tech geeks?

Bitcoin can seem confusing at first, for it works in a way different than most currencies and payments systems. The technology and economics behind it can be daunting. However, the same could be said for other popular technologies, such as email and social media. Very few people could explain the technology behind how email works, but just about everyone knows how to use it. Bitcoin may not be as user-friendly as email yet, but it is quickly developing such that understanding what's happening "behind the scenes" won't be necessary for using it.

    The purpose of this book is to give a basic understanding of Bitcoin for non-technical people, so hopefully after you have completed it, it won't seem so confusing!

BITCOIN AS A PAYMENT NETWORK

9. How is Bitcoin a payment network?

The Bitcoin network, called the "Blockchain," is a sophisticated electronic payment network that allows people to exchange bitcoin, the currency (note the lowercase "b" to distinguish the currency from the entire Bitcoin network). The Blockchain is an online ledger that records all transactions on the Bitcoin network and prevents people from sending or receiving bitcoins fraudulently. What

> Refer to *Bitcoin as Currency* for questions about the Bitcoin currency.

is revolutionary and unique about the Blockchain is that it allows people to transfer a currency electronically without any need for a trusted third party, such as a bank or credit card company. Although there have been other digital currencies in the past, or ideas for digital currencies, Satoshi's unique invention of the Blockchain allows for a practical method of exchanging digital currencies safely and efficiently.

10. Why is it called the "Blockchain?"

The Bitcoin payment network is called the Blockchain because all transactions are grouped in "blocks" that are "chained" together all the way back to the first block ever created. Because all transactions ever completed in Bitcoin history are linked, and these transactions are stored on computers throughout the world, no one is able to go back and falsify previous transactions.

11. How does the Blockchain work?

Every time someone transfers bitcoins to another person, the transaction is transmitted to the Bitcoin network. When a new block (group of transactions) is added to the Blockchain, the new transaction is included and is thus recorded on the Bitcoin network. For example, if Alice sends 3 bitcoins to Bob at 10:59 AM on 9/9/2015, their transaction is permanently recorded on the Blockchain, which lets the whole network know that Alice no longer has control of those bitcoins, and that Bob now has control of them.

12. Where does the Blockchain reside?

The Blockchain is stored on every computer in the world that is running a full "node" on the Bitcoin network. Anyone can run a Bitcoin node. This is what makes Bitcoin decentralized, and it prevents any one person or organization from taking control of the Bitcoin network. There is no centralized command center which would be vulnerable to attack.

> See the question "What is a Bitcoin node?" later in this chapter for a discussion on nodes.

13. Is the Blockchain secure?

The design of the Blockchain makes it incredibly secure. Blocks are added to the Blockchain by means of Bitcoin "mining."

> Mining will be described in the chapter *Bitcoin Mining*.

Each block contains many transactions, and each block is connected to the chain of previous blocks. The way the process works, the longer a block has been on the Blockchain, the more secure it is. This is because each block added confirms the validity of all the blocks before it.

Imagine someone stacking 1,000 pound weights, one on top of the other. It would be incredibly difficult to lift the top weight off the stack. But imagine if the stack contained 500 weights, and you had to lift the top 300! The Blockchain is designed so that the deeper the Blockchain gets, the more secure it is.

Furthermore, Bitcoin uses what is called "public-key cryptography" to ensure that transactions

> See the chapter *Using Bitcoin* for a further explanation of Bitcoin's use of public-key cryptography.

themselves are not forged. This is an advanced method of encryption that prevents someone from taking control of someone else's bitcoins or pretending they are someone they are not. Also, the existence of all the previous transactions on the Blockchain ensures that a person can't "double-spend."

14. What does it mean to "double-spend" bitcoins?

"Double-spending" means sending the same bitcoins to two separate recipients. This is prevented by the process of confirmations on the Blockchain. For example, if Alice sends 3 bitcoins to Bob, and then 20 minutes later she tries to send those same 3 bitcoins to Carol, the Blockchain will see the first transaction and then reject the second one, since Alice no longer controls those bitcoins.

15. What is a Bitcoin node?

A "node" is simply one of the computers running the Bitcoin software that transmits transactions throughout the Bitcoin network. Nodes transmit only those transactions that are considered legitimate

See the chapter *Ownership of Bitcoin Network* for more discussion of Bitcoin protocols.

transactions – ones that conform to the Bitcoin protocol. Nodes also store an entire copy of the Blockchain locally, syncing it constantly with the rest of the network. By storing the entire Blockchain in each node, the Bitcoin network is highly resistant to attacks and attempts to shut it down. Just one functioning node is all that is necessary to keep the network alive. As of September 1, 2015, there were over 6,000 nodes active on the Bitcoin network around the world.

Note that the Bitcoin network is non-hierarchical; in other words, there is no node more important than any other node. Any node can propagate transactions to the network, and each node picks up transactions from other nodes and propagates them further.

16. What is a Bitcoin confirmation?

Aside from regular nodes, specialized nodes called "miners" run on powerful computers and add groups of transactions to "blocks" on the network. This process is called a Bitcoin "confirmation."

BITCOIN AS A PAYMENT NETWORK

After Bitcoin nodes have validated a transaction and transmitted it to the Bitcoin network, a miner node will add the transaction to a future block, thus confirming the transaction. A confirmation means that the transaction has been accepted by the Bitcoin network.

> See more on mining in the chapter *Bitcoin Mining*.

It is common parlance in Bitcoin to say that a transaction has "multiple confirmations." This means that the transaction has been added to a block (1 confirmation), and then additional blocks have been added to the Blockchain after that block. Each added block in a sense confirms all the blocks before it. So let's say Alice's transaction was added to block #201. When block #202 is added, her transaction will have 2 confirmations; when block #203 is added, it will have 3 confirmations, etc. The more confirmations a transaction has, the less likely it is that it could be fraudulent, since each additional confirmation further validates the transaction. However, even a transaction with just one confirmation is highly unlikely to be fraudulent, as the act of adding each block entails a sophisticated method of validating transactions.

17. How long does it take to confirm a transaction?

A Bitcoin transaction is usually instantaneous, much like sending an email. However, to prevent the possibility that the transaction is a double-spend, most merchants wait until the transaction is confirmed on the Bitcoin Network before accepting it. Each confirmation takes, on average, up to 10 minutes. For small purchases, such as a cup of coffee, a merchant could accept the transaction without any confirmations, but for a larger purchase most experts recommend around 4-6 confirmations, which can take up to an hour to occur.

18. An hour seems like a long time to validate a transaction – how can that be practical?

Two things to consider: First, when a transaction has received 6 confirmations, it is completely and totally validated. By comparison, a typical credit card transaction can take up to 90 days to be fully cleared – chargebacks are still possible during this time.

Second, as was mentioned above, smaller transactions can occur with many fewer confirmations (or even no confirmations). Further, entrepreneurs are currently working on other ways to confirm transactions more quickly in a way satisfactory to both merchants and consumers.

19. Are there any other uses for Blockchain technology?

Absolutely. Technology experts see many possible uses for a technology like the Blockchain. A decentralized online ledger whose security is insured by mathematics could be used for validating contracts, keeping track of stock ownership, recording any type of financial transactions, and a plethora of other applications.

BITCOIN AS CURRENCY

20. How is Bitcoin a currency?

A currency is anything that is used as a medium of exchange. Instead of a barter system where I trade what I own for what you own, currency allows us to buy and sell our items for a commonly-accepted unit of measurement: $3 for a gallon of milk, $10 for a pound of steak, etc. Bitcoin includes within it a currency, called "bitcoins." Like any currency, people can own, spend, and receive bitcoins from other people. However, unlike most currencies, bitcoins are the first widely-used currency that is completely digital.

21. Are there different denominations of bitcoins?

Just as there are different denominations of government-issued currencies (such as dollar, quarter, dime, nickel, penny), so there are different denominations of bitcoins. The biggest denomination is the "bitcoin," which (obviously) equals 1 bitcoin. Currently each bitcoin can be divisible to eight decimal places, i.e., 0.00000001 bitcoins. This smallest denomination of bitcoin, one-hundred millionth bitcoins, is called a "satoshi," in honor of Bitcoin's creator. Thus, there are one hundred million satoshis in one bitcoin. Also, it is common to refer to 0.000001 (one millionth) bitcoins as a "bit." So there are a million bits in a bitcoin.

There has been some debate about naming other denominational amounts of bitcoins, but currently the three most accepted denominations are the bitcoin, the bit, and the satoshi. Most Bitcoin users agree that eventually other denominational amounts will need to be named in order to make the use of Bitcoin more friendly. It is much easier to say, "I'm sending you 200 bits" rather than "I'm sending you 0.0002 of a bitcoin."

22. How are bitcoins created?

Approximately every 10 minutes a set number of bitcoins are added to the Bitcoin network. This happens through a process called "mining." Of course when we say bitcoins are "created," we do not mean that physical coins are created. What it means is that more bitcoins are available on the Bitcoin payment network.

> Mining will be described in the chapter *Bitcoin Mining*.

23. How many bitcoins are there in existence?

The number of bitcoins on the Bitcoin network is being increased approximately every ten minutes. However, the Bitcoin network is configured to add a deceasing number of bitcoins over time. By the year 2140 a total of 21 million bitcoins will have been generated and the process of adding bitcoins will stop. As of September 1, 2015, there were approximately 14,560,000 bitcoins.

> The question of why only 21 million bitcoins will be created is answered in the chapter *Economic Advantages of Bitcoin*.

24. What is the symbol for Bitcoin?

Like any currency, Bitcoin is designated with a particular symbol. The most commonly used symbol for bitcoins is ฿ (an upper-case B with two vertical lines through it). Many devices are unable to render this symbol, so other symbols have been proposed, although none have been adopted on a widespread basis by Bitcoin users. It is also typical to use the abbreviation "BTC" to refer to a bitcoin, so, for example, if a person has 4 bitcoins, he could write that he has "4 BTC" or ฿4.

OWNERSHIP OF BITCOIN NETWORK

25. Who owns the Bitcoin network?

No one person or organization owns the Bitcoin network. Like the Internet it is built upon, Bitcoin is *decentralized*, and no single entity controls how it operates or how bitcoins are distributed and spent. This is unique in modern-day currencies, all of which are created and controlled by governments. The running and development of Bitcoin is based upon consensus, meaning that the users of Bitcoin decide how it will operate and function.

26. If Bitcoin is decentralized, then what does control Bitcoin?

Bitcoin is controlled by certain protocols that govern all the operations of the network (much like the Internet is controlled by specific protocols). These protocols determine how bitcoins are added to the network, the process by which bitcoins are transferred from one person to another, and all the other rules necessary to run the Bitcoin network.

27. Does anyone control these Bitcoin protocols?

The Bitcoin protocols are controlled by *consensus*. Any proposed change requires that the majority of Bitcoin users support that change in order for it to be integrated into the network.

For example, let's say someone proposes that instead of creating a total of 21 million bitcoins, the network should create 100 million bitcoins. If that person were to make that change in his version of the Bitcoin software, it would have no impact on the rest of the network unless others decided to implement it also.

However, the fan of 100 million bitcoins does not have an incentive to make this change if there is not consensus behind it. Why? If he alters his version, his changes would create a new network, called a "fork." This fork would become incompatible with the main Bitcoin network, and the currency on the fork would become worthless, since no one would use them.

When a change is made to Bitcoin protocols, it is done by a team of core developers who maintain the Bitcoin software. Minor changes such as bug fixes are made by them without any real controversy. However, sometimes a major change will be proposed, and Bitcoin users disagree as to the benefits of this change. In these cases, the process of consensus can be ugly and messy, with heated debates between the two sides of the issue. This might seem inefficient, but it is really democracy at work. Only changes that are acceptable to most Bitcoin users will be implemented. Users "vote" for what they want by their choice of which version of the software they use. Change is implemented when most users choose a version that has incorporated the change.

28. Can these decentralized, free protocols really work?

Some people find this decentralization unsettling. We assume that there needs to be one "voice" in a project in order to avoid anarchy and chaos. But this is not true in real life. Think about language. No one "created" English, and no one is in charge of maintaining it, yet we obviously have the ability to communicate with each other. This has occurred by way of millions of people coming to agreement about how we communicate. No centralized authority has maintained the language.

Bitcoin decentralization works because all users of the Bitcoin network are incentivized to come to consensus. If there is no consensus, then Bitcoin fragments and becomes worthless to its users. Thus, the users of Bitcoin work to ensure that consensus is reached.

TECHNOLOGICAL ADVANTAGES OF BITCOIN

29. What are the technological advantages of Bitcoin?

Bitcoin is a modern, advanced payment network that is far superior to existing payment networks that were created before the Internet. Two of the main advantages of Bitcoin are that (1) it greatly reduces the chance of problems such as identity theft and credit card fraud; and (2) it greatly increases the ease of payments. Bitcoin is a payment network created from the ground up for an Internet Age.

30. How does Bitcoin address credit card fraud?

Our current credit card payment systems use technologies that were created before the invention of the Internet and were never intended for use online. Although many people use their credit cards online without major problems, this apparent serenity is a false one that is propped up by billions of dollars of support from financial institutions – dollars that ultimately are charged to the consumer (i.e., you and me).

31. How is the consumer charged for credit card fraud?

It is now standard policy that a customer is not responsible when his credit card is used fraudulently. So if someone purchases $500 worth of items from an online retailer with a stolen credit card, the legitimate owner of that credit card doesn't have to pay that $500. Yet, $500 was spent – so who pays for it? In most cases, the bank eats it as the cost of doing business. However, these fraudulent charges add up to billions of dollars (one study in 2009 estimated $190 billion in the United States alone), and banks don't truly absorb those costs.

Instead they make up for them with credit card fees that retailers pay. If you spend $100 with your credit card at a store, typically the store only gets about $97-98, and the bank receives the difference. Again, this doesn't seem like a problem for the customer, as it is the retailer who eats the cost. However, retailers take into consideration these fees when they set their prices; they must mark up their prices to cover the credit card fees they have to pay. And who pays those prices? The consumer. So expenses related to fraud totaling billions of dollars every year are added to the cost of purchasing things, simply because the payment system is inefficient at preventing fraud.

32. Why is the credit card payment system so open to fraud?

One of the biggest flaws in our current credit card payment system is that the buyer gives away access to her entire account every time she buys something. You input your name, address, and all credit card details – number, expiration date, and the card security code – just to order a $10 book online. In other words, you expose everything a malicious person needs to access all the money in your account. Although this is the norm today, it is highly insecure, as can be seen from the many credit card breaches that occur in both online and brick-and-mortar stores.

33. How is Bitcoin superior to this credit card payment system?

Bitcoin uses a completely different model for payment, one that is more like cash. When you transfer bitcoins to another person, all you give him are those specific bitcoins. He has no way to access any more of your bitcoins. You don't even have to give him your name or contact information if it is not required for the purchase. It's just like giving a $20 bill to the cashier – but it can all be done electronically. Bitcoin, however, also works like cash in that it is non-reversible: once you transfer those bitcoins, there is no way to get them back unless the other party agrees to send them to you.

34. How does Bitcoin address ease of payments?

Since the system is based completely on mathematical protocols and

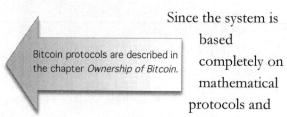

Bitcoin protocols are described in the chapter *Ownership of Bitcoin*.

strong encryption, the transfer of bitcoins can be done instantaneously and securely over the Bitcoin network. The process does not need human intervention and costs as much as sending an email – i.e., a negligible amount.

Although we don't realize it as consumers, credit card transactions actually take weeks to clear. Further, sending any large amount of money electronically (say, over $10,000) is an expensive process that takes days to complete. Bitcoin can send any amount of money instantaneously and usually for less than a few cents.

ECONOMIC ADVANTAGES OF BITCOIN

35. What are the economic advantages of Bitcoin?

The underlying economic model of Bitcoin is significantly different than government-issued currencies like the US dollar or the euro. Because of this, it has certain advantages over those currencies, the primary three being that it does not require a trusted third party to validate transactions; it is not subject to government control of the money supply; and it is truly global in reach.

36. What is meant by a "trusted third party" for validating transactions?

Imagine your typical financial transaction. You order something on Amazon, and input your credit card information when checking out. Even though this transaction is just between you and Amazon, there is a third party involved. For how do Amazon and other retailers know that your credit card is valid, and that you have the appropriate funds to cover the cost of the purchase? On their own, they do not. They trust financial institutions (banks and credit card companies) to verify this.

Even when you pay for something with cash, a third party is involved – the government backing the currency. For the merchant trusts that the amount represented on the bill – $1, $5, $20 – is what that piece of paper is actually worth. But if the government decides to increase the supply of money, that piece of paper has a decreased purchasing power.

37. What's wrong with having to trust a third party for financial transactions?

Many times having a third party behind a financial transaction works just fine. But this is not always the case, for when you must trust a third party, you don't have total control of your money, and you don't have real freedom. For example, currently there are many government officials and economists around the world who advocate abolishing, or at least greatly limiting, the use of cash. There are already strict limits on how much cash a person may withdraw from her own bank account, and many merchants will not accept cash for large purchases because of restrictions from their financial institutions. Further, in countries that have oppressive governments, the "trusted" third party is often under government control (or is the government itself), and so any transactions not approved by that government are rejected – and possibly even grounds for arrest.

38. How does Bitcoin remove the need for a trusted third party?

When a transaction occurs on the Bitcoin network, the validation of the transaction is made by the network through the use of mathematical calculations and cryptography. The validation does not depend upon an organization or government being involved in the transaction.

> See *Bitcoin as a Payment Network* for more details about Bitcoin validations.

39. Why is government control of the supply of money a problem?

Government control of the supply of money makes the value of that money subject to the arbitrary whims and desires of government officials, who are typically concerned with short-term problems. This has led to all government-controlled currencies losing value over time. Since the creation of the Federal Reserve – the central bank of the United States – in 1913, the value of the US dollar has dropped over 96%. In other words, a dollar today can only buy you about 4/100th of what it could buy you in 1913. This has been a consistent decline over the past 100 years – for example, a dollar today can only buy you about 35/100ths of what it could 35 years ago. Consider the following chart, which shows how many loaves of bread could be bought with $10 over the past 100 years:

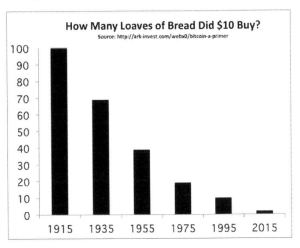

The dollar buys fewer loaves of bread each year since 1915.

This dramatically decreasing value of the dollar is the result of inflation, which is an increase in the supply of money.

In theory, wages will also increase (although increased wages often lag behind increased prices of goods), but the decreasing value of the dollar is a problem because it means that the money you make today – your wages – will be able to buy less the longer you hold on to it. So a dollar earned today is worth 98 cents next year. This encourages you to spend your money perhaps when you don't want to, since the money diminishes in value the longer you hold it. It also makes it very difficult to save for the long term – say, for retirement – because every year you hold onto your money it has less buying power.

40. Isn't it government's role to issue money?

Not really. Many people think money and the State are intrinsically linked, but there is no reason they need to be. In fact, some would argue that it would be better if the State had nothing to do with money, since then it couldn't just print more whenever it couldn't raise "enough" through taxes. One constant in the history of government-issued money is that it always ends up becoming worthless. Always.

41. But didn't governments create money?

Contrary to popular belief, money did not originate with the State. Evolving from barter, certain commodities were seen to have good traits for a method of exchange: easy to divide, transportable, durable, and fungible (one unit of the currency is worth the same as any other unit). As a commodity (often gold or silver) became accepted for exchange, governments began to create currencies using those materials. It was not a king who said, "Let this be money!" – it was the decisions of countless people in real life (the "market") that decided what made the best money.

42. Why does an increase in the supply of money lead to a decrease in the value of a dollar (rising prices)?

Imagine the following scenario: Alice and Bob both have $100, and they both want a new bike that Carol is selling. Alice is willing to pay $90, but Bob will give his whole $100 for it. Carol will sell it to Bob in that case, assuming she is most concerned about how much money she gets back. What if both Alice and Bob, however, were to get a gift of another $100 from their grandmothers? Now Alice might come back and offer more than $100, knowing she would still have some money left. Bob, on the other hand, wants the bike more than money, and so he might be willing to go up to $200 now. In any case, the increase in the money supply resulted in a higher price to pay for the bike. Of course in a sophisticated economic system like that of the United States this process is a bit more complicated, but the basic logic is the same: increasing the money supply results in increasing prices.

43. Why are rising prices bad?

Rising prices mean that the money we earn can't purchase as much as it could in the past. This penalizes us for saving, since money we hold decreases in value over time. Common sense indicates that saving money for the future is not something that should be penalized in a healthy economy.

44. How does Bitcoin address the issue of inflation and rising prices?

In the Bitcoin network, there will never be more than 21 million bitcoins in existence at any time. There is no way for a government or

> See *Bitcoin Mining* for more information on how bitcoins are created.

corporation to change that number – the only way it can be changed is if the community of people using Bitcoin come to consensus and agree to change it (something very unlikely to happen). With a fixed money supply, rising prices for goods become much harder to achieve; in fact, usually the same goods will cost less over time. According to the creator of Bitcoin and its proponents, this is good for everyone.

45. Won't having a currency that goes up in value keep people from spending it?

Some argue that if people own a currency that goes up in value over time, they will be hesitant to spend that currency. If, for example, $100 can buy a desk today, but in two years it could buy two desks, then supposedly people will hold on to their money waiting for that better deal in the future. However, an example can show that this is not what happens: consider the electronics industry.

Over time, electronic devices, such as computers, tablets, and smartphones, have gotten more powerful while also becoming cheaper. In effect, this is what would happen in all industries if the currency itself went up in value (i.e., prices would go down) Yet people still purchase electronic devices, and lower prices do not prevent that from happening. There are certain purchases that everyone must make (food, shelter, clothes, etc.), but by having a rising value (or steady value) of one's currency, a person can be free to spend or invest without being worried about the declining value of her savings.

46. Is Bitcoin limited to one country or a small number of countries?

Unlike modern government-issued currencies, Bitcoin's reach is truly global. No government controls it, and since it is not connected to any country's currency, it reaches to every part of the globe. This means that money can be transferred between countries with no need for a currency exchange or costly fees. A bitcoin is worth the same in Austria as it is in Zimbabwe.

47. Are there any other economic advantages to Bitcoin?

Being a currency that is independent of any government or organizational control, Bitcoin is not subject to easy manipulation by global powers. For example, since the Bitcoin protocol sets the supply of bitcoins, there is no way for more bitcoins to be created during a crisis, which is what usually happens with government-controlled currency. History shows that when a country wants to go to war with another country and can't afford it through taxes, it creates new money. When it wants to institute a social program and can't get support for raising taxes, it creates new money. When they have control of the money supply, even democratic governments are able to engage in behavior that is against the will of the people and yet paid for by the people.

> Refer back to *Ownership of Bitcoin* for a discussion of Bitcoin protocols.

USING BITCOIN

48. Why should I use Bitcoin?

Bitcoin is in many ways superior to traditional currencies and payment networks. It may be difficult to get started using Bitcoin, but once a person uses it, she sees how much easier, cheaper, and convenient it is to use than credit cards or even cash. Some jokingly refer to Bitcoin as "Internet Magic Money" because it is so different from our antiquated payment systems that it seems to work like magic. For a society that does most of

> See *Technological Advantages of Bitcoin* and *Economic Advantages of Bitcoin* for many of the benefits of using Bitcoin.

49. How do I store bitcoins?

Bitcoins are stored in something called a "Bitcoin wallet," software that can run on a computer or other electronic device (phone, tablet, etc.). Bitcoin wallets are protected by a password that you set when you first install the wallet. This password must be kept safe and secret; it gives complete access to the wallet and all bitcoins stored in it.

50. How do Bitcoin wallets work?

Bitcoin wallets keep track of the transactions on the Blockchain, allow you to send the bitcoins that you have control over, and permit you to receive bitcoins from other people. Some wallets are also nodes, storing a full copy of the Blockchain on the device, but many wallets – such as smartphone-based wallets – are not, only keeping track of the minimum information needed to access the Blockchain.

Technically, a person doesn't "own" bitcoins,

> See *Bitcoin as a Payment Network* for a discussion of the Blockchain and Bitcoin nodes.

he *controls* them. Without getting too bogged down in the details, what a wallet really stores is your "private key" which gives you access to certain bitcoins (or fractions of a bitcoin) – the ones you control. When you pay for a good or service, you transfer control of certain bitcoins from yourself to the other person.

51. What is a private key?

A private key is what allows you to control certain bitcoins, and what keeps anyone else from controlling them. It is called a "key" because it unlocks bitcoins for your use. A private key is simply a long alphanumeric string. However, in most wallets the private key does not need to be memorized, just the wallet password. The wallet stores the private key in an encrypted fashion and uses it for those who can access the wallet (i.e., those with the wallet password). A private key is always linked to a "public address" on the Bitcoin network.

52. Why are private keys important?

The most important thing to remember when it comes to storing bitcoins is that *anyone who controls your private keys controls your bitcoins!* Giving someone access to your private key is like giving him or her the key to your house – it comes with complete control over everything the key unlocks.

53. What is a public address?

A public address is what is used to receive bitcoins. It can be likened to an email address (i.e., me@mail.com) that people need in order to send you email. Like a private key, a public address is a long alphanumeric string – such as "1K65tkPwZD67WdC1xUqi5aJkeoyS6oiJdK." While you keep your private key secret, your public key can be seen by anyone (and in fact needs to be seen by people so that they can send you bitcoins!).

54. How are a private key and public address related?

Private keys are linked to public addresses through something called "public-key cryptography." Using complex mathematics, these strings are generated such that someone can easily confirm that a public address is linked to a private key if they know the value of the private key, but it is almost impossible for someone to know the value of the private key even if they know the public address. As a simple analogy, consider the following equation:

$$415x^3 - 391x^2 + 132x = 20{,}832$$

If I asked you what "x" is, and you have to answer within a few seconds, it will be very difficult. But if I tell you that x=4, then it will only take a few seconds to confirm. Public-key cryptography uses advanced mathematics to create a problem that even the most powerful computers can only solve one way. This allows someone with a private key to easily access the bitcoins associated with the corresponding public address, but it is impossible for someone knowing just the public address to access those bitcoins. Note that the computations necessary to link private keys and public addresses is all done behind the scenes and the typical user doesn't need to understand it or even know it is happening.

55. Where do I get a Bitcoin wallet?

Bitcoin wallets can be downloaded from the main Bitcoin website, www.bitcoin.org, and smartphone-based wallets can be installed from the Apple and Android stores. In addition to downloadable wallets you install on your device, there are also online wallets, in which all information associated with your wallet is stored on a remote server. Another option is hardware wallets, which are small devices that can be connected to your computer and are dedicated to securely storing, spending, and receiving bitcoins.

> See *Resources* at the end of this book for a list of various Bitcoin wallets.

56. What if I lose my Bitcoin wallet password?

Losing a password to a Bitcoin wallet means that you lose access to that wallet and all the bitcoins it controls. There is no way to recover the bitcoins from that wallet without your password. This is both an advantage and a disadvantage: it means that no one can access your wallet without your password, but it also means that without it, neither can you.

57. Can I backup my bitcoins?

Yes, a Bitcoin wallet can be (and should be) backed up. If your computer crashes and everything on the computer – including your

Bitcoin wallet – is lost, you can restore that wallet from a backup and your password. The various wallet software have differing ways of handling backups, but usually backing up your wallet entails copying a certain file to another device.

58. How can I secure my bitcoins?

The first thing to do to secure your bitcoins is to have a strong, secret password on your Bitcoin wallet. However, since your wallet resides on your computer, if your computer is hacked, then it is possible that someone could steal your bitcoins (for example, if a hacker installs a program to record you when you type your password). For this reason, most experts recommend storing any large quantities of bitcoins on "paper wallets."

59. What is a paper wallet?

We saw that bitcoins are controlled through private keys and public addresses. These are simply long strings of letters and numbers, and these strings can be recorded on a piece of paper and then stored in a safe place. Since these private keys/public addresses are not stored on a computer, they cannot be hacked and your bitcoins stolen. Storing your bitcoins in this manner is called having a "paper wallet." Another term for a paper wallet is "cold storage." Most Bitcoin wallets include an import function that allows you to bring the cold storage bitcoins into your wallet when you want to access them.

60. How do I send people bitcoins?

In theory, sending bitcoins is as easy as sending an email. In your wallet software, you enter two pieces of information: the public address of the person to whom you wish to send bitcoins, and the amount to send. Then press "Send!"

61. Is it really that easy to send bitcoins?

Not exactly. In practice sending bitcoins can currently be likened to sending email in the early 1990's – it can be cumbersome and confusing. Although much development has occurred in this space over the past few years, sending bitcoins can still be a challenge to the novice. The public addresses are the most user-unfriendly part of the process. Since they look something like this – "1K65tkPwZD67WdC1xUqi5aJkeoyS6oiJdK" – they are not exactly easy to remember or input into wallets for sending.

62. Can the sending process be made easier?

Many companies are working on making sending bitcoins easier. Currently, the most common way to simplify these addresses is through the use of "QR Codes." These are images that look like this:

You can scan a QR Code with a smartphone, which then automatically enters the public address. Many QR Codes also include the amount to send as well as a label noting the purpose of the payment.

Going forward, this is one of the main areas for improvement before we can expect greater adoption of Bitcoin.

In 1992, very few people knew how to send email. In 2000, most young people could. By 2010, most older, non-tech-savvy people could as well, due in large part to the significant interface improvements in email programs. We are likely to see a similar adoption cycle (although probably shorter) for sending and receiving bitcoins.

63. What if I send my bitcoins to the wrong address?

If the address entered in a Bitcoin wallet is an invalid address, i.e., one that is impossible on the Bitcoin network, then the wallet will typically give an error message and not send the bitcoins. However, if it is a valid address, the bitcoins will be sent. Whenever bitcoins are sent to a valid address, the transaction is permanent – it cannot be undone.

64. How do I receive bitcoins?

First, you give the person or organization who wishes to pay you your public address, either in its long string form (such as "1K65tkPwZD67WdC1xUqi5aJkeoyS6oiJdK"), or as a QR Code. Once someone sends bitcoins to your address, they will shortly appear in your Bitcoin wallet – usually as quickly as an email,

See *Bitcoin as a Payment Network* for an explanation of Bitcoin confirmations.

65. How do I get bitcoins?

If you are interested in using Bitcoin, the best thing to do is to convert some of your government-issued currency (i.e., dollars, euros, etc.) to bitcoins. A number of businesses let you do this, and they all work similarly: you enter your bank account information, and then purchase bitcoins. These companies usually also supply online "wallets" in which you can keep your bitcoin, but most experts recommend that users keep their bitcoins in their own wallets on their computers or smartphones. If you do this the bitcoins are truly under your control. The easiest wallets for storing smaller amounts of bitcoin – i.e., spending money – are those for your smartphone.

> See *Resources* at the end of this book for sites that allow you to buy and sell bitcoins and others that offer wallet software.

Another way to acquire bitcoins is by offering goods or services in exchange for them. There are also services that allow part of your paycheck to be paid in bitcoins, no matter who you work for. Finally, you can mine bitcoins, but this has become a relatively expensive endeavor that is mostly reserved to large Bitcoin mining companies.

66. What is a Bitcoin exchange?

A Bitcoin exchange allows people to exchange their bitcoins for other currencies, usually both other cryptocurrencies as well as government-issued currencies. Typically, a user will link her bank account information to the exchange to deposit her government-issued currency at the site; then she can buy, sell and trade bitcoins as well as the other currencies.

Exchanges are really only for those who wish to trade bitcoins on a regular basis – it is not necessary for the person who just wants to use Bitcoin for buying and selling goods and services.

Unfortunately, the history of Bitcoin exchanges has been checkered. Many have

> See the chapter *Security of Bitcoin* for a discussion of the security of Bitcoin itself vs. the security of exchanges and individual wallets.

been hacked, gone bankrupt, or had their owners disappear with users' funds. In many exchanges, the bitcoins in a user's account are actually under the control of the exchange (i.e., the exchange has the private keys), which means, of course, the exchange actually owns the bitcoins.

67. Who accepts bitcoins?

Since the first "real-world" Bitcoin transaction in 2010, the number of merchants accepting Bitcoin has increased exponentially. Some prominent companies that accept Bitcoin include Dell, Overstock, and Expedia. Furthermore, at some sites you can purchase gift cards with bitcoins that can be used at stores like Amazon, Target, and Walmart.

68. What are some other ways Bitcoin can be used?

Bitcoin can be used in many of the same ways that credit cards, cash, and wire transfers are used. However, there are certain uses for which Bitcoin is particularly suited. For example, remittances to foreign countries – when a person sends money back to family or friends in his native country – are tailor-made for Bitcoin. Instead of expensive, slow and cumbersome methods of moving money to other countries (such as wire transfers), Bitcoin provides a cheap, quick and efficient way to move money.

Furthermore, there are approximately 2.5 billion "unbanked" people in the world. A weaver in rural India only needs a smartphone (many of the "unbanked" have inexpensive smartphones) and she would be able to control large quantities of money. People in the developing world could leap-frog traditional payment systems (which don't work well for them anyway) and move directly into 21st century payment systems.

Bitcoin offers many advantages over first-world payment systems, but the real potential for the cryptocurrency is in those parts of the world that traditional payment systems do not serve well.

COST OF USING BITCOIN

69. How much does it cost to use Bitcoin?

Most Bitcoin wallets can be downloaded for free. Further, anyone can run his own Bitcoin node on a personal computer. Users pay no fee to receive bitcoins from other people, but the sender pays the small fee associated with each

> See *Resources* at the end of this book for sites that allow you to download a Bitcoin wallet.

> Refer back to *Bitcoin as a Payment Network* for questions regarding Bitcoin nodes.

bitcoin transaction.

70. What is the fee the sender pays for transferring bitcoins?

The size of the fee is currently negligible – equivalent to a few cents – regardless of the size of the transaction. In other words, someone could send millions of dollars worth of bitcoins across the world and only pay the equivalent of a few cents to do it. The fee itself is variable and is set by the sender. The size of the fee can determine how quickly a transaction is added to the Blockchain (i.e., "confirmed"). The higher the fee paid, the quicker it will be added, although currently even a fee worth just a few cents will get a transaction confirmed within minutes.

> See *Bitcoin Mining* for questions regarding mining and block rewards.

71. Who collects the fees?

Fees are added onto a transaction, and when a miner confirms that transaction in a block added to the Blockchain, she receives the fee along with the block reward. For example, if I send 3 bitcoins to someone, my wallet will add the fee (perhaps .0001 bitcoins) to the transaction. That fee will then be collected by the miner who includes that transaction in the next block added to the Blockchain.

72. What if I don't include a fee in my Bitcoin transaction?

It is possible to send bitcoins to another address without including a fee. If this occurs, the most likely result is that the transaction will be delayed before being confirmed on the Blockchain. This is because miners will not be incentivized to include it in a block, since they receive no fee to do so. It is still possible it will be confirmed, but it might take hours, or even days.

BITCOIN MINING

73. What is Bitcoin mining?

Bitcoin mining is the process by which new bitcoins are added to the Bitcoin network; it is also the process which secures the Bitcoin network. It is called mining because Bitcoin was consciously designed to emulate precious metals such as gold and silver, and just as "adding" new gold and silver to the world's supply is called mining, so too this is the name for adding new bitcoins to the world's supply. And, as with precious metals, the supply

> See *Bitcoin as a Currency* for a discussion of the total number of bitcoins to be added to the Bitcoin network.

of bitcoins is limited and no government can control this supply.

The average user doesn't have to understand mining in order to use Bitcoin in daily life. However it is an essential aspect of Bitcoin; mining keeps the Bitcoin network secure and ensures the orderly addition of new bitcoins to the network.

74. How does Bitcoin mining work?

One of the potential problems with a digital currency is security. Before Bitcoin, most attempts at securing a digital currency involved a central control center that validated transactions and protected the network from hacking and attacks. However, a centralized design like this is fragile for several reasons: a government agency can simply shut it down by closing that control center; hackers can focus on one location for attacks; and there is a single point of failure (i.e., the command center) for the whole network.

Bitcoin solves the problem of securing the network in a completely different way. Instead of a centralized control center managed by one organization, Bitcoin involves disparate people all over the world in a process called "mining." In this process, powerful computers, owned by mining companies or even individuals, compete to solve sophisticated mathematical problems, with the winner receiving a set number of bitcoins determined by the network. The purpose of this competition is to secure the network, for it prevents people from confirming bad transactions or counterfeiting bitcoins, and the reward for participating in this competition is new bitcoins. Thus, people all over the world have an incentive to participate in making the Bitcoin network more and more secure.

The process is complicated, but essentially the power needed to solve these problems, along with the combined power of all the computers attempting to solve these problems, makes it almost impossible to create fraudulent Bitcoin transactions. If someone wanted to do so, they would need more computing power than the majority of the Bitcoin network, which is substantial and growing every day. In fact, the cost to "overpower" the Bitcoin network is far greater than the potential benefits of doing so.

75. How often are new bitcoins added to the Bitcoin network?

The Bitcoin network is designed such that these mathematical problems are solved approximately every 10 minutes (if problems are being solved too quickly, they get harder, and if too slowly, they get easier).

76. How many new bitcoins are added each time bitcoins are mined?

The number of bitcoins awarded for mining steadily decreases over time. The initial "block reward" was 50 bitcoins. It was reduced in half to 25 bitcoins in 2012, and will be halved approximately every four years (every 210,000 blocks, to be exact). By the 2030's most bitcoins will have been added to the network, as can be seen in this graph:

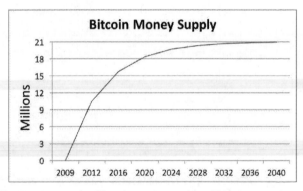

The Bitcoin network adds a decreasing number of bitcoins over time.

77. How long will new bitcoins be added to the network?

Around the year 2140, all bitcoins will have been mined and there will be no more mining award.

78. Why weren't all 21 million bitcoins released to the network at once?

When Satoshi Nakamoto created the Bitcoin network, he intentionally set it up so that bitcoins would be added slowly over time. This was done for a few reasons:

1) If all bitcoins had been added when the network was created, then a handful of people could have owned them all, which would have discouraged anyone else from using Bitcoin.

2) By allowing bitcoins to be the reward for mining, there is now an incentive for disparate people across the globe to secure the network.

3) The gradual addition of bitcoins over time exhibits a control over the money supply similar to precious metals, which makes each bitcoin more valuable during the time before Bitcoin becomes mainstream.

79. Can I mine bitcoins on my computer?

When Bitcoin first began, it was possible to mine successfully on any standard personal computer. But as the Bitcoin network has grown, the difficulty of the mathematical problems to be solved has greatly increased. As a result, one needs a specialized computer to mine bitcoins, and usually the energy and computer costs involved make it unprofitable for an individual to mine. Most mining is now done in "pools," in which many people group together their resources and share the block reward.

80. What will happen after new bitcoins can no longer be mined?

At that point, the only way to make money mining will be on the fees associated with each bitcoin transaction. However, most experts believe that the growth of the network by then will ensure that mining will still be a profitable endeavor for those who engage in it.

ANONYMITY OF USING BITCOIN

81. Is Bitcoin anonymous?

When Bitcoin first became known outside of the technical world, it was often called an "anonymous" network – you could spend bitcoins on something without anyone tracing the purchase back to you. However, to paraphrase the cliché, "Reports of Bitcoin's anonymity have been greatly exaggerated." As can be imagined, a network that records every single transaction is not truly anonymous. It is more accurate to say that Bitcoin is "pseudonymous."

82. What does it mean that Bitcoin is pseudonymous?

Bitcoin is meant to be cash-like, and when you spend cash you don't ordinarily have to reveal your personal details to the merchant. Likewise, when you spend bitcoins, there is no obligation to reveal your identity as you must with credit cards. Although when you spend bitcoins you can assume another identity, if anyone links you to that identity, they will know that you spent those bitcoins. Remember: the Blockchain records every transaction and chains them together – that's what prevents "double-spends." So every transaction of bitcoins from one address to another is logged and recorded. Theoretically, one could trace the chain linking every transaction ever recorded in Bitcoin history.

> Refer back to *Bitcoin as a Payment Network* for an explanation of "double-spends."

83. How could a person's bitcoin transaction be traced back to her?

Let's say Alice wants to use bitcoins to buy a

software download online that she doesn't want anyone to know about. So she creates an account at the site with a false identity, and buys the product with her bitcoins. However, the bitcoins she spends are ones that she purchased from a Bitcoin exchange using her real identity. If someone were willing to put in the many hours necessary to do so, they could connect those transactions and know that Alice was likely the person who purchased that product.

> Refer back to *Using Bitcoin* for a discussion of what a Bitcoin exchange is.

Bitcoin is superior to credit card transactions in that a person doesn't have to give all his personal details every time he wants to buy a cup of coffee. But it is not truly anonymous and no one should consider it so.

SECURITY OF BITCOIN

84. Can I use Bitcoin securely?

No financial payment system is 100% secure. In any traditional system of financial transactions, there are various ways security can be breached, which we have all seen exposed in the news. Examples include the massive hacks, bank robberies, and other thefts that have occurred over the years. Some of the weak points in traditional payments systems include these: the security of banks – both the buildings that hold currency as well as the network security that prevents hackers; the security of the merchants who record and store transactions; the physical security associated with owning a credit card; and the security practices of the individuals that use the currency. On the other hand, Bitcoin security has only two points of potential failure: the security of the Bitcoin network itself, and the security of individual wallets that hold bitcoins.

85. Can the Bitcoin network be hacked?

The Bitcoin network is incredibly secure – that's one of the strongest benefits of it. The Blockchain contains all transactions ever recorded in Bitcoin history, and it is stored on thousands of computers worldwide. Trying to alter those transactions for one's benefit would take computational power that would cost far more than the possible payoff. Furthermore, the encryption used to secure each individual transaction is as powerful, if not more powerful, than the encryption used by major financial institutions and banks. If the encryption underlying Bitcoin were to be broken, the world would have many more financial problems than Bitcoin fraud to worry about.

86. Can Bitcoin wallets be hacked?

Since wallets are created by various software developers, and operated by individuals, they are open to hacks, just like any software. As Bitcoin is currently used, all responsibility for the security of one's bitcoins lies with the owner. This decentralizes the risk: a hacker would need to hack countless wallets to obtain the same amount of money he could obtain by hacking one bank or credit card company. However, if an individual uses a poorly-designed wallet, or does not secure his private key, or has her computer where the wallet resides hacked, or generally doesn't follow good security procedures (strong passwords, etc.), then it is possible that his bitcoins will not remain in his possession for long. In an era where most security obligations fall on financial institutions, many people are not ready for this level of responsibility. Fortunately, many companies are continuing to develop Bitcoin wallets that are more and more easy-to-use as well as easy-to-keep-secure.

87. Are there any other ways I can lose my bitcoins?

The most likely way a person can lose her bitcoins is by trusting her private keys to a third party, such as an online wallet or Bitcoin exchange. Using an online service like these can be beneficial in that it puts the responsibility on a supposed "expert" in security instead of the novice, but it can be very, very bad when that third party is incompetent, immoral, or both. In the short history of Bitcoin, more than one exchange and online wallet have lost users' funds. This has led some people to conclude that Bitcoin itself is insecure. However, it was not the Bitcoin network that was the problem, but those who were trusted with other people's bitcoins.

88. What is the best way to keep my bitcoins secure?

Because it resides completely on the Internet, standard security practices for Internet security are applicable to Bitcoin: using strong passwords, keeping passwords in a safe place, securing your device against viruses and hackers, and two-factor authentication where applicable. Further, those who use online wallets and exchanges should only keep small amounts on those sites, as you don't control the private keys of those bitcoins. Finally, any large amounts of bitcoins should be kept mostly in paper wallets to prevent hackers from stealing them.

> Refer back to *Using Bitcoin* for an explanation of paper wallets and Bitcoin security procedures.

VALUE OF BITCOIN

89. What is the intrinsic value of a bitcoin?

A bitcoin's value is what people decide its value is. This might seem like a circular argument, but really it is not. The "intrinsic" value of any currency – whether it be dollars, gold, or yen, or any commodity, such as potatoes, iron, or bubble gum – is whatever people are willing to give up for it. The reasons behind why we value something might vary (backing of government, properties of the item, ability to be used to make something else, etc.), but no matter the reason, the value of anything is whatever two or more people agree to. Bitcoin's value comes from the efficiency of the network as well as the limited supply of bitcoins.

90. But Bitcoin isn't physical; can it really have an intrinsic value?

Sometimes when people talk about "intrinsic" value they are thinking of some physical property an item has. For example, gold has value because it can be used in electronics and is popular for use in jewelry. But anytime somebody wants something, it has value – and if two people want something, the value can be described more accurately as the highest price someone is willing to pay to obtain it.

Coming back to Bitcoin, people have decided that it has value because it is an easy and cheap way to transfer wealth. If another, far superior, method of doing what Bitcoin does comes along in the future, then most likely Bitcoin's "intrinsic" value will plummet to zero. But as long as people find it useful, it has value. Just like every currency and commodity.

91. Won't 21 million bitcoins be too few for billions of people to use?

A common misperception of currency is that you can have too little of it. For example, some would argue that if you have 100 million people in a society, then having just, say, 10 million units of currency in that society would be unworkable. There wouldn't be enough for everyone to use. However, this is not the case. That society could have any quantity of currency, *as long as the currency is sufficiently divisible.*

92. What does it mean to say a currency must be sufficiently divisible?

Let's consider the situation mentioned above (100 million people/$10 million). If all the money were equally divided among the people, then everyone would have 10 cents ($10 million divided by 100 million people). That could never work, correct? But what if the smallest-sized coin wasn't worth 1/100 of a dollar (i.e., one cent), but was worth 1/1,000,000 of a dollar? Let's call that denomination a "tiny." In that case, every person in this equitable society would have 100,000 "tinys." It should become clear then that a pack of gum could go for 1 tiny, a gallon of milk for 10 tinys, etc.

93. How divisible is Bitcoin?

Currently, Bitcoin is divisible to the eighth decimal place (.00000001); the smallest unit of Bitcoin is called a "satoshi," after the creator of the cryptocurrency. So if I own 1 bitcoin, I own 100,000,000 satoshis, and eventually there will be 21 quadrillon satoshis available in the entire Bitcoin network. If the value of one bitcoin continues to rise, a book might cost a few satoshis, while a car could cost a few thousand. No matter how much or how little one bitcoin is worth, it is capable of being used for transactions of any size.

Also note that the current divisibility of Bitcoin could be increased in future updates to the network, so the possibilities are infinite.

> Refer back to *Bitcoin as Currency* for a discussion of the different Bitcoin denominations.

OBJECTIONS TO BITCOIN

94. Is Bitcoin "real"?

People have a hard time accepting as valid a currency that they can't hold in their hands. "If you can't hold it, you don't own it" say some people, especially the proponents of precious metals. And in the case of precious metals, there is much wisdom in that saying. Even when talking about a government-issued currency like the US dollar that is mostly used electronically, many people instinctively have the same attitude. In the back of their minds is the notion that in an emergency they could always just cash out all their savings and investments and put all the cash under their mattresses. (In reality, of course, most financial institutions won't let customers withdraw large amounts of cash.)

Yet in many ways Bitcoin is actually easier to truly "hold" than most forms of currency, especially government-issued currency. With Bitcoin, if you have control of the private keys, then you have complete and total control of the bitcoins. There is absolutely no way another person can get them unless you give them up (either through bad security, by force, or voluntarily). All of your money at the bank, however, isn't really yours – it is actually owned by the bank, and the bank agrees to give it back to you if you ask for it…with a number of stipulations (like the limit on withdrawals).

The non-physicality of Bitcoin is a problem mostly of psychology. As physical beings, we like to be able to touch and feel and see before we consider something "real." You can't do any of this with Bitcoin. Yet it can be used as currency to purchase items, so it truly is as real as any other currency.

95. Isn't Bitcoin just for thieves and drug-dealers?

From its early days, Bitcoin has been associated in the public eye with criminal activities. And it is true that many criminals have used Bitcoin in their illegal dealings. But do you know which currency criminals prefer more than any other worldwide? The US dollar in the form of cash. Because Bitcoin has properties similar to cash, it can be used like cash for nefarious purposes. In fact, every currency that has ever existed has been used for criminal purposes – the problem is the criminals, not the currency. All that heightened criminal activity proves is that a currency is popular and easy to use – exactly what we want in our currency, correct?

96. Why is the price so volatile?

When Bitcoin burst into mainstream knowledge, one thing it was noted for was its price volatility. In 2010, you could obtain bitcoins for almost nothing. By the end of 2013, they were worth over $1,200 per bitcoin, and they hover in the $200's as of this writing. Isn't this a sign of an unstable currency, or at least some underlying problem?

The truth is that Bitcoin is still very young and somewhat experimental. No one knows exactly how it will be used in the future or how much it will be used. So determining its value is going to be a volatile endeavor. As people understand and use Bitcoin more, it is likely that the price will greatly stabilize (and it already has to some degree).

97. Isn't Bitcoin illegal in some countries?

The legality of Bitcoin has been contested in several countries, including the United States. Some opponents of Bitcoin have argued that only the government has the right to create a currency, and therefore any privately-created currency, such as Bitcoin, is illegal. However, in March 2014, the United States Internal Revenue Service declared that for tax purposes bitcoins should be treated as a commodity, which implies their legality – how can you tax something that is illegal to own?

Governments in countries such as China and Russia have at times made negative statements regarding Bitcoin, but many of these statements are conflicting and/or confusing. At the time of this writing, owning bitcoins is illegal in only a handful of countries, and more and more countries are explicitly declaring it legal to own and use them.

THE FUTURE OF BITCOIN

98. What will Bitcoin be like in the future?

Bitcoin is an exciting technology that clearly has great potential to change the way people use money. However, it is still essentially an experiment. As such, it could one day be replaced by a better technology, or found to have a major technical flaw. The latter is unlikely, since the network has been used for millions of transactions already, but the former is always a possibility. Furthermore, governments might decide that the use of Bitcoin threatens their power structures and pass laws restricting its use. Although many bright minds and a lot of money are being directed towards the expansion of Bitcoin, it cannot be guaranteed that it will ultimately succeed in the marketplace.

99. Is buying bitcoins a good investment?

Since Bitcoin is still young and experimental, there is no way to know what the price of bitcoins will be in the future. This book is focused on Bitcoin as a payment system, a currency, and a technology; it takes no position on Bitcoin as an investment. Many believe that the price of bitcoins will increase over time, due both to its greater usage and its decreasing supply, but no one can predict the future.

100. Will Bitcoin replace the dollar?

Probably not. Eventually the dollar will fail, because all government-issued currencies fail. It might be replaced by Bitcoin, the yen, or some other currency; there is no way to know. It might be replaced by a cryptocurrency other than Bitcoin that hasn't even been invented yet, or by a hybrid government-issued cryptocurrency.

101. Will the Blockchain replace our current credit card payment networks?

Although it is unlikely that Bitcoin will replace government-issued currencies completely, it is more likely that the Bitcoin network could replace, or at least greatly enhance, traditional credit card payment networks. Financial institutions have noticed the inherent efficiency and low-cost maintenance of the Bitcoin network, and many of these institutions are looking seriously at the Blockchain to see if its principles can be applied to their own networks.

CONCLUSION

In the past twenty years we have seen the incredible growth of communications technologies. From sending a text-based email via mainframe terminal to having instant access to friends and family through texting, email, and social media, the growth in our ability to communicate with others easily and quickly has been tremendous – and unprecedented in the history of the world.

Many people today are asking if the financial world might see the same kinds of dramatic changes in the next few years. Although most of our financial dealings are now online, the payment networks we use are based on pre-Internet technologies that have many inherent weaknesses. Further, the dramatic manipulation of government-issued money supplies has devalued our currencies and made individuals' money subject to the whims of those in power. In many ways, the financial world is due for a radical makeover.

Is Bitcoin that makeover? There is no way to know for sure, but at the very least Bitcoin has allowed people to look at money and how they use it in a whole different light. Even if Bitcoin is not the solution to all the problems of the financial world, it is pointing us in the right direction: a payment network and currency that are decentralized, owned by no one and thus by everyone, and incredibly secure.

If you are not yet using Bitcoin, I encourage you to do so. This book has given you the knowledge and tools necessary to engage this 21st century payment network and currency – now you just need to get started!

RESOURCES

Information about Bitcoin

www.bitcoin.org - The official Bitcoin site where one can download the "Bitcoin Core" software in order to run a Bitcoin node. It also includes various tutorials and documentation regarding Bitcoin.

www.bitcoin.com - Useful site with information to help create a wallet, buy bitcoins, follow Bitcoin news, and participate in online discussions about Bitcoin.

Selected Bitcoin Wallets

Desktop

- Bitcoin Core – www.bitcoin.org (runs a full node, but is also a desktop wallet)
- Multibit – www.multibit.org
- Armory – www.bitcoinarmory.com

iOS

- Breadwallet – www.breadwallet.com
- Airbitz – www.airbitz.co
- Copay – www.copay.io

Android

- Mycelium – www.mycelium.com
- Airbitz – www.airbitz.co
- Copay – www.copay.io

Hardware

- Trezor – www.bitcointrezor.com
- Ledger – www.ledgerwallet.com

Online

Online wallets are in reality more like Bitcoin "banks." They allow you to store your bitcoins on their site, but you don't have full control over them as you would with a wallet on your device. The benefit of online wallets is that they are the fastest and easiest way to obtain bitcoins: all you do is link your bank account information, and they will allow you to buy and sell bitcoins through their site.

- Coinbase – www.coinbase.com
- Circle – www.circle.com

Paper Wallet/Cold Storage

Paper wallets are the most secure way to store your bitcoins, but are usually only used for long-term storage, as bitcoins stored on a paper wallet cannot be easily sent. Creating a paper wallet involves the manual generation of a public/private key pair, which must be done properly or the key pair could be insecure. The website below will securely create a public/private key pair for you. A hardware wallet (see above) is recommended for large amounts of bitcoins if you need to access your bitcoins frequently.

BitAddress – www.bitaddress.org

Updated Information

New wallets are added to the marketplace frequently. Occasionally older wallets become unsupported. For updated information on what is available, please go to www.ericsammons.com/bitcoin-resources.

ACKNOWLEDGEMENTS

I would like to thank Tom Woods and Erik Voorhees, who first made me enthusiastic about Bitcoin.

I would also like to thank my wife Suzan, who patiently helped edit this book, and made it much more readable than my original draft. Any lingering mistakes are mine alone.

Also, thanks to my children Lucy, Maria, and Peter who gave important input to make the text more clear and readable.

ABOUT THE AUTHOR

Eric Sammons is the author of several books, including a high school textbook on world religions. He holds a degree in Systems Analysis with a concentration in Economics from Miami University in Ohio, and earned a Master of Theology degree from Franciscan University. He worked in the software development field for more than 15 years, including 10 years as the owner of his own software firm. He is a freelance writer and editor.

Eric and his beautiful wife Suzan have seven children. They currently reside in Florida and are serious baseball fans.

Eric's website "Swimming Upstream" may be found at www.ericsammons.com.

INDEX

A

alt-coin 8
anonymity............................ 71

B

backup............................ 52, 53
Bitcoin exchange 58, 73, 77
bits 22
Blockchain..11, 12, 13, 14, 15, 16, 17, 19, 48, 62, 63, 72, 76, 89

C

cold storage .. See paper wallet
confirmation 16, 17, 18
consensus 25, 26, 27, 28, 43
credit card fraud 29, 30
criminal purposes 85

D

decentralization.............. 27, 28
denomination................. 22, 81

divisible 22, 81, 82
double-spend 15, 18

E

exchange .... See Bitcoin exchange

F

fee 61, 62, 63

G

government control .8, 35, 37, 38

I

identity theft......................... 29
inflation........................... 39, 42
intrinsic value 79, 80
investment............................ 88

L

legality 86

INDEX

M

mining 6, 14, 23, 58, 65, 66, 68, 69, 70
money supply 8, 35, 42, 43, 45, 69

N

node 13, 15, 16, 17, 61, 93
number of bitcoins .. 23, 67, 68

P

paper wallet 54
private key ... 49, 50, 51, 77, 95
protocols 8, 26, 27, 32
pseudonymous 71, 72
public address .. 49, 50, 51, 54, 55, 56
public-key cryptography 14, 50

Q

QR Code 55, 56

R

remittances 59

S

Satoshi Nakamoto 6, 69
security . 19, 31, 66, 75, 77, 78, 84
symbol 24

T

trusted third party 7, 12, 35, 36, 38

U

unbanked 60

V

volatile 85

W

wallet 48, 49, 51, 52, 53, 54, 56, 63, 77, 93, 94

Made in the USA
Monee, IL
22 October 2021